THE NEW GRAD'S GUIDE TO FINANCIAL SURVIVAL

Michael A. Shockling

CONTENTS

INTRODUCTION

You just graduated, or maybe you soon will. You started a new job or maybe are thinking ahead, or maybe you've been working for a bit. You have your talents, your skills, and you're ready to make what you can of it. This place can financially crush you, or you can make it work for your benefit. Learning how to do the latter will only take a little time.

This is intended to be a simple roadmap to guide your personal and long-term financial security. It is assumed that you do *not* want to dedicate long hours studying accounting, tax laws, investment theory, macrocconomics, and financial history. But it's also assumed that you're interested in making the best decisions to help you avoid financial problems down the road.

Well…good news! You can be equipped with the knowledge to make the financial decisions that serve your interests with just a little bit of effort! No degree needed, no long-winded thesis on stock valuation or weeks absorbing the expert advice on CNBC. Just the basics and some common sense. It turns out to be very simple.

We'll go over the most important topics. You can, and maybe should, dig deeper for the information needed to make your personal decisions as they come. All in due time. But the early years of your financial life will have a disproportionally huge impact on your wealth in later years, as we'll soon explain. You can make some simple and well-informed decisions to set yourself up for success later.

The goal here is to cover the basics of almost every topic you need to start heading down the path toward maximizing your wealth. Very soon, you will be equipped with enough knowledge to be your own financial advisor for a very long time. In the coming years, you'll want to investigate detailed topics on the finer points, but for now we'll keep it simple, because that's all you need to do.

Let's dive in!

CHAPTER 1: WHAT IS NET WORTH?

Let's assume you'd rather be wealthy than poor. Wealth means how much you have which is yours and nobody else's. Wealth can be measured by adding up the value of your **assets**. Something which is yours that is worth something and can be converted to cash for acquiring other things is an asset and can be assigned a value. A $10 bill is an asset and is sometimes called a "liquid" asset because it's very easy to move around and use (spend). A house is also an asset, but it's not liquid because you can't easily use it or spend it on a meal.

But sometimes we owe money. Or, things we own require a continued money supply. These are **liabilities** and they have a negative effect on our wealth. An example of a liability is any kind of loan which is owed. Credit card debt (say, a $10 balance owed on a credit card) is a liability not only because it is money owed to someone else, but also because they will expect you to pay them interest until the money is paid back. So you owe $10 today and you'll owe another few dollars a month from now, perhaps.

Net worth is simple to calculate:

Net Worth = Assets – Liabilities

Can we see how to maximize wealth? Maximize assets and minimize liabilities!

Let's look at an example. Imagine you have a house worth $1M with a mortgage (loan) for it through which you still owe the bank $500k. You also have a stock portfolio of $500k. We'll tabulate this with negative values for liabilities in parentheses. In accounting, this tabulation of assets and liabilities is called a **balance sheet**:

Assets	
Home	$1,000,000
Stock portfolio	$500,000
Liabilities	
Mortgage	($500,000)
Net Worth	$1,000,000

Congratulations! You're a millionaire! Can you stop working and are you set for life?

Maybe, but not so fast. Imagine you spend $50k per year to eat and clothe yourself, move around the world...whatever. You have 10 years of somewhat liquid assets (the stock portfolio) saved up. Are you going to live longer than that? To determine whether your savings will keep up with your spending and affect your net worth over time, you need to look at your <u>income</u>.

Income statements assess the amount of income (money coming in to increase your net worth) and expenses (money going out to decrease your net worth) incurred over a period of time. If you currently have positive net worth, it's the result of some amount of time in the past when you had more money coming in than going out. If you have negative net worth, it's the result of some time with net negative income.

Let's say you graduate high school and land a great job. You spend the first year living in your parents' basement, mooching off their food and borrowing their car. You earn $40k that year. You live it up with your friends and spend $5k over the course of the year on your favorite activity attending basket weaving shows. Ignoring everything else, here's the income statement for that year:

Revenues	
Job	$40,000
Expenses	
Basket Weaving Hobby	($5,000)
Net Income	$35,000

Over this first year, you will have increased your net worth to $35k by having $35k in positive net income. You made yourself wealthier over the course of the year!

Now let's say you are feeling ambitious and see yourself being a heart surgeon one day. You need to go to school! You will have tuition, room, and board, and you won't be able to work. What does that look like?

Revenues	
Job	
Expenses	
Basket Weaving Hobby	($5,000)
Tuition, Room, and Board	($30,000)
Net Income	($35,000)

Holy moly! You're in the hole $35,000! That's $70,000 worse off than when you lived in your parents' basement! Is college bad?!

No, not necessarily, as we'll see later in Chapter 4. College earns you an intangible asset which allows you to increase your future earnings. You voluntarily take on negative income for a few years in exchange for much larger positive income in later years. Taking on debt (liabilities) to become a heart surgeon is probably a decision which will help your financial security in the long run, assuming you fulfill that dream. Paying ivy league tuition to get a degree in basket weaving is probably not.

So we want to have positive net income, meaning we earn more than we spend. And we want to ultimately have positive net worth, which means having more assets and fewer liabilities. It turns out that we need to be careful about the *kinds* of assets and liabilities we acquire, because they affect more than just your wealth today…they affect your wealth in the future.

CHAPTER 2: ASSETS AND LIABILITIES

In addition to your job, your assets and liabilities can affect your net income. Some day, you could accumulate enough assets that they generate more income than your job! On the other hand, with enough liabilities, you might need to work two jobs just to earn enough money to pay for your liabilities. So it's important to understand the difference to make sure we're on the right path from the start.

Assets

We can think of an asset three different ways: (1) an **appreciating** asset, which becomes more valuable over time, (2) a **neutral** asset, which holds its value relatively steady, and (3) a **depreciating** asset, which loses its value over time.

Appreciating assets are arguably the only thing that we should call **investments** because they involve us setting aside resources and deferring our own consumption for the specific purpose of having more resources in the future. Appreciating assets are the engine driving individual wealth, earning you wealth while you sleep. The growth in value of these assets is expected based on the **fundamental value** of what they represent growing over time. "Fundamental" here means some tangible, quantifiable reason. Not because someone else might like it better some day and pay you more like a rare baseball card or some digital image of a monkey. Examples of appreciating assets with fundamental value include:

-      Stocks (shares in a company which give us rights to the company's earnings now and in the future)
-      Bonds (loans to companies or municipalities which pay a fixed interest)
-      Treasuries (loans to the federal government which pay a fixed interest)
-      High yield savings (cash in the bank paying low interest)

The assets above are listed in order from riskiest to least risky. Typically the riskiest ones have the largest growth potential, but that comes at the expense of certainty. Stocks can lose *all* of their value if the company goes bankrupt, but can also grow dramatically and with no upper limit as the profits of the company grow (think Apple, Amazon..). Bonds have a fixed interest rate which will be paid, no more and no less, unless the company, municipality, or government completely fails in a catastrophic way. Savings accounts pay a low interest rate and are guaranteed (insured) by the federal government. We will cover investments in more detail later, where it will be clear why these increase in value in "fundamental" ways.

Neutral assets are designed to hold their value as stores of wealth with little or no appreciation or depreciation, as the fundamental value of what they represent does not change. Examples include:
-      Cash under your mattress
-      Real estate (your house)
-      Precious metals (gold, silver)
-      Cryptocurrencies (but beware!)

These assets are listed in order from the most to least stable. Technically, cash depreciates at the rate of **inflation**, which is a measure of how the price of things changes over time relative to a fixed currency. As things get more expensive over time, your cash can buy less. Historically inflation is less than a few percent per year, but in bad times or in third-world countries with bad policymakers, it can significantly erode the purchasing power of your cash and savings.

Real estate tends to track inflation over time, but historically has experienced large temporary or local fluctuations due to economic influences. If companies undergo a large hiring wave in a region with limited land and housing (think San Francisco), prices can climb fast. Conversely, if everyone is losing their job, prices can fall (think Detroit). Fundamentally, the range of cost and value for a typical family home will never reach zero except in rare circumstances where there is local economic collapse, and it will never reach a value of 100 times the median worker salary except in rare circumstances where there is a local economic boom and external non-resident investors pour in. Usually there is a range of reasonably achievable cost that the market will bear.

Precious metals and cryptocurrencies are loosely similar to each other. They produce nothing and do not physically change over time, so there is no reason why they should be worth more or less in the future than they are today...they in fact have no fundamental value relative to currency. Precious metals could arguably have a minimum value based on their industrial use. For example, gold is used for plating of materials and platinum is used in automobile exhaust systems, so even if nobody is buying the material as a store of wealth, its value is nonzero.

Cryptocurrency, on the other hand, has no use outside of being a "currency" which is not backed by any government and is not legal tender (required to be accepted as payment). There is no fundamental reason why cryptocurrencies have any value at all. History shows it is not "neutral" in the sense that it is a stable store of its value; in fact the various cryptocurrencies have shown far more price volatility than even stocks. You should treat cryptocurrencies as a slightly better use of your money than lottery tickets. Don't be surprised if the value goes to $0, and consider yourself lucky if the value increases.

Metals and cryptocurrencies are argued by some to be a more stable store of wealth than slightly depreciating government currency (cash). But both suffer from speculative investors, supply and demand fluctuations, and other forces which in practice can generate extreme volatility, not stability.

And then there are depreciating assets, which are likely to lose their value over time. These are magnificent destructors of your net worth. Unfortunately, these are the things that most people want! Examples include:
- Cars, boats, and vehicles
- Clothes
- Electronics
- Personal jewelry
- Furniture and stuff

Almost everything you "buy" can be considered a depreciating asset. That $100,000 Tesla sure makes you look rich today, but sometime in the future it will be all used up and worth $0. It's actually making you poor! That $3,000 leather sofa? That new iPhone? That fancy end table? Those designer jeans? Someday they'll be worthless.

Now we can understand how (1) appreciating assets gain value and/or pay you money, produce net positive income, and increase your net worth, (2) neutral assets maintain value and should not change your net worth, and (3) depreciating assets lose money, are equivalent to negative income, and decrease your net worth.

So: Purchases of "investments" make you richer over time. We'll see more in Chapter 5 why that is the case. Buying piles of gold bars does not; in the long run it likely neither makes you richer nor poorer. And purchases of visible displays of wealth actually make you poorer.

Liabilities

Liabilities for personal financial purposes can be loans resulting from purchases which are too large or simply inconvenient for us to make with cash. They can also result from purchases made with money we simply don't have (credit card debt). All liabilities in isolation are bad. Some are less bad. You want the least bad ones, and only the ones which are absolutely necessary. That's the liabilities topic in a nutshell.

Think about a car loan. You're buying a depreciating asset, which is already going to make a dent in your net worth over time by losing its value and being equivalent to negative income. Let's say you buy a $10k car for $10k cash. At the time of the transaction, your net worth is not affected at all because you have spent $10k but you've acquired a $10k asset. In 5 years you hope to maybe sell it for $5k. You'll lose $5k in net worth over that time, or $1k per year. Not terrible…it's the cost of doing business to keep that magnificent job across town that you love.

Now imagine you don't have $10k in cash, but you really need the car to keep that job. What do you do? You get a car loan. You take on $10k in liability at the time you acquire the $10k asset… again, no net change to your net worth on the day you buy the car. Now let's say the car dealer says, "no problem, you can buy this car for $1k down and $191.22 per month for the next 5 years." They've extended you a loan to cover $9k which you aren't paying up front, and the **annual percentage rate (APR)** of the loan is 10%. Super affordable!

Great! So what you've done is you've added a $10k (depreciating) asset to your balance sheet as well as a $9k liability (after paying $1k). However, the dealer is getting some interest on the loan they've given you, so you will have some negative income associated with paying the interest in addition to paying off the loan itself. At this rate of $191.22 per month, you'll pay a total of $11,473 to the bank over 5 years in addition to the $1k you put down. Effectively, you'll have paid $12,473 for the car, which means you'll be out $7,473 when you sell the car for $5k in 5 years. That's almost 50% more damage to your net worth than if you had just paid $10k on day 1!

You can go online and use one of many free interest calculators to explore these types of situations. Here we used the formula for calculating the payment on a loan:

$$Payment = Loan \times \left[\frac{\frac{r}{12} \times \left(1 + \frac{r}{12}\right)^t}{\left(1 + \frac{r}{12}\right)^t - 1} \right]$$

where r is the % APR and t is the number of months

Now, let's imagine you can get a 0% loan instead of a 10% loan. You'll pay $9k back for the loan at $150/mo., which results in the same as if you had paid $10k on day 1 and a net worth reduction of $5k. So if you need that car loan, make sure the care is cheap and the rate is as low as possible.

What did we learn? Owing money at interest is not good! And the higher the interest rate of your loan, the worse it is for you!

Other liabilities can be even worse than car loans. Think about credit card debt, which can have rates upward of 20-30%. Imagine you use a credit card to buy plane ticket for $300, which we can assume depreciates eventually to $0 for simplicity. You buy it on a credit card with a 25% rate and pay it off over 3 years. You end up actually paying $429 for it!

A liability need not be a loan from a bank to put a drag on your wealth. Think about smartphones. Free iPhone with any 3-year contract, right? Well, bad news: this is a loan in disguise. You're paying for that phone one way or another, and it will depreciate fast! And, the contract just might be structured such that you're effectively paying interest on the "loan" for the phone in addition to what you'd need to pay for the cell service. Read the fine print, calculate the total cost, and shop around; you may be able to have phone service for much less over that 3-year period with a different contract structure.

How terrible a liability is will depend on the asset it is associated with and its rate. In order from least to most terrible:
- Student loans: Rates are typically low and may be government subsidized. The loan is associated with an education which can lead to higher future cash flow.

- ◦ Exception: A high rate loan for a financially useless degree can be terrible.
- Mortgage: Rates are typically only slightly higher than inflation and the expected appreciation of the home value. Income tax benefits exist. Home ownership can be an asset (more on this later).
  - ◦ Exception: A high rate mortgage on a house in a temporarily inflated region can be terrible if you need to sell the house after its price drops.
- Car loan: Manufacturers often provide very low rates as purchase incentives. But the underlying asset depreciates.
- Credit cards: Extremely high rates, no underlying asset to speak of…the Tyrannosaurus Rex coming to clobber your net worth.

So after understanding the concept that appreciating assets can increase wealth and liabilities decrease it, next let's figure out how to forecast the effects of our choices on our future net worth.

CHAPTER 3: ASSET GROWTH AND OPPORTUNITY COST

Almost everything in finance deals with money and time. The concept that an investment made today could be worth more in the future underpins all of accounting, finance, and business strategy. It's why you invest, and it's why the credit card companies want you to rack up big credit card debts.

Appreciating assets increase in value **exponentially**. Not in the figure-of-speech sense, but in the mathematical sense. Here's why.

Imagine you loan money to the government in agreement for a 3% interest payment upon return of your money in a year. You give them $1, and in a year they'll give you $1.03. Then you do it again the next year. You give them $1.03, and they give you back 3% more of that...around $1.06. If you keep reinvesting at 3%, you'll have $1.34 after ten years.

The formula for this **exponential growth** is:

$$Future\ Value = Principal \times (1 + rate)^{time}$$

You probably learned this years ago. But the magic of <u>compounding interest</u>, where your investment can grow according to this exponential formula such that the growth is proportional to the current value, is the motivation for you to invest and invest as soon as you can. Every year, the amount your investment grows is more than the previous year.

Imagine instead of 3%, our investment can grow at 7%, right around the long-term average for the broader US stock market. Well in 10 years, our $1 will be worth $1.97, around double. This is a useful rule of thumb to remember: 7% growth per year will approximately double your money in 10 years.

Just to get the point across, let's see what this looks like in Fig. 3-1 at the 7% rate. On the top, we see how the amount that the value increases grows with time. From year 19-20 alone, the growth is $0.25, 25% of your initial investment! On the bottom, we plot the same data but with the y-axis on a logarithmic scale. On this type of plot, if the values increase in a straight line, it confirms that there is exponential growth. We will use this type of plot to determine if real data is growing exponentially.

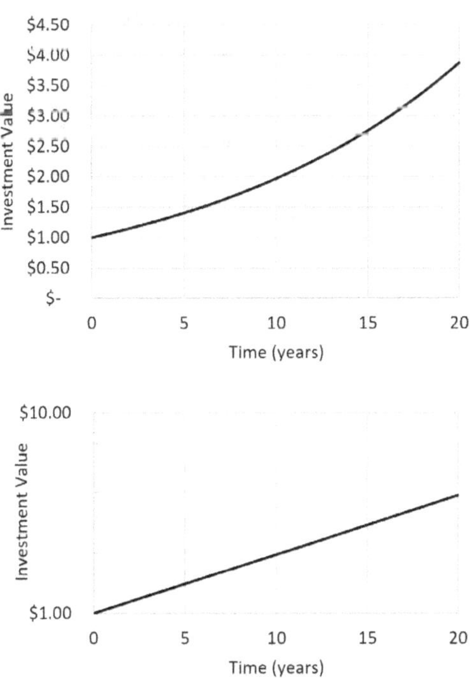

Fig. 3-1 Exponential Growth of an Investment

So let's look at the Gross Domestic Product (GDP) of the US economy. The GDP is basically the value of everything produced by everybody in the US. It's used by economists as a proxy for economic progress; as we all make more, we all have access to more, we all earn more money, and our standard of living improves.

The US GDP is shown in Fig. 3-2. The top figure shows the upward-curving data, and the bottom figure plotted on a logarithmic y-axis shows approximately a straight line. This is exponential growth all the way back to 1947!

Why?

Every year, GDP tends to go up by a few percent on average. During rough years, like the 1970s or during economic recessions, the rate slows a bit or even becomes negative (meaning we produce less in a year than in the year prior). During boom times, the economic productivity gains are a bit larger and it steepens. Over this 76-year period, GDP grew from around $0.2 trillion to over $27 trillion, an increase by a factor of 113. This averages to around 6.4% per year...so the US economy has been growing exponentially for the last 76 years (and more)!

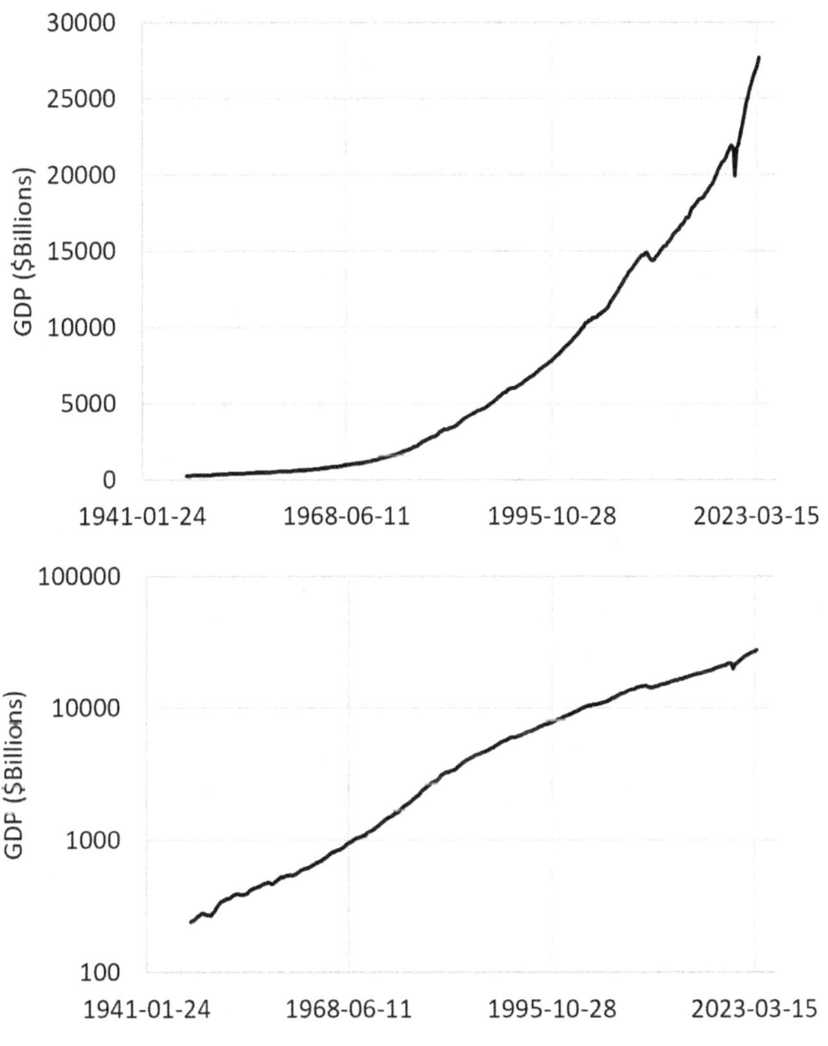

Fig. 3-2 US GDP from 1947 to 2023

The point of all of this is to show that there is a rational reason to expect exponential growth from your investments. As we all go to work and incrementally improve our productivity, invent new things, optimize processes, and even grow in population, GDP grows incrementally year over year.

Now consider this. You're 20 years old and have $1,000. You imagine you'd like to own a fancy car to cruise around with your fancy friends. Can you purchase one today with $1,000? Absolutely not. But if you invest that $1,000 and wait 60 years until you're 80, growing exponentially at 7% per year, your investment will be worth $57,946! That's a Cadillac!

Or even better, maybe you're dead set on being a millionaire someday. Here's a secret: you can be, and it's not out of reach. In fact, it's completely realistic, almost to the point of being a sure thing. It just takes regular investments and some time.

Let's say you've worked a couple summer jobs and pinched pennies and have $3,000 to invest. Fantastic! Go out and open an account and invest in a broadly diversified US stock fund (we'll talk about that in Chapter 6). Easy. Now for the slightly more difficult part: commit to continue investing $400 a month. $4800 a year. Sound hard? $13 a day? Does it really sound that impossible when the average monthly car payment in 2023 is over $700 a month? This might not be *easy*, but it's not so unimaginable that only the top 1% could fathom it.

We can use easy math to predict the future value of regular periodic investments (this is called a **regular annuity**) in addition to using the previous formula for the future value of the initial $3,000 investment. The formula for the regular investments is:

$$Future\ Value = Amount \times \frac{(1 + rate)^{time} - 1}{rate}$$

In this example, the investment *amount* is $400, the *time* is the number of months, and the *rate* is the monthly growth rate (the yearly rate of 7% divided by 12).

If you have the financial discipline to invest $3,000 at age 20 and continue to invest $4800 per year ($400 per month), growing your investments at 7% per year, your account will be worth $1,003,172 by the time you're 60 years old. At that point, your investment will be earning you $70,000 a year! In your sleep!

The power of compound interest and exponential growth comes

from the element of *time*. In the example we just covered, you start saving at age 20. The table below shows the value of your investment if you start this disciplined investing later. The amazing thing to notice here is that if you start investing at age 20, over 50% of your net worth at age 60 is defined by the investments you make in the first ten years! If you wait until you're 30, you'll be less than half as wealthy. And if you wait until you're 50, building much wealth at all will be very difficult.

Age Starting Investments	Value at Age 60
20	$1,003,172
30	$476,249
40	$208,387
50	$72,220

In fact, we can determine how much money you'd need to regularly save to make it to $1,000,000 by age 60, assuming a 7% investment growth rate. In the table below, we see again that you need to save more than double the amount if you start at age 30 rather than 20.

Age Starting Investments	Monthly Amount Needed to Reach $1M at Age 60
20	$417
30	$882
40	$2,033
50	$6,031

Are you convinced yet that "now" is always the best time to start investing rather than later??

So we've discussed how investments grow, and we've shown the power of exponential growth of appreciating assets through compounding interest. Now let's think about depreciating assets. In contrast to growing their value with time, depreciating assets lose value over time. The formula is the same, just with a negative rate, resulting in **exponential decay**. Imagine an asset which depreciates 10% per year, maybe a car. If it starts at $1, after year 1 it's $0.90. After year 2, it's $0.81, and so on.

We can apply these simple concepts to explore a basic decision's impact on our net worth: we have $20,000 to either invest or to use for buying that car we want for commuting to work. Suppose our investment can grow at 7%, and the car depreciates at 10%. What's the effect on our net worth 20 years later?

Fig. 3-3 illustrates the stark contrast. The investment grows (as we know from the 7% rule of thumb) to about 4 times its original size to nearly $80,000; it doubles in 10 years, and doubles again in another 10. The car after 20 years is worth a little under $2500. This might be optimistic, actually, depending on the car.

That lady taking the bus to work? It might not be because she can't afford a car...it's because she is saving her money and putting it to work for her!

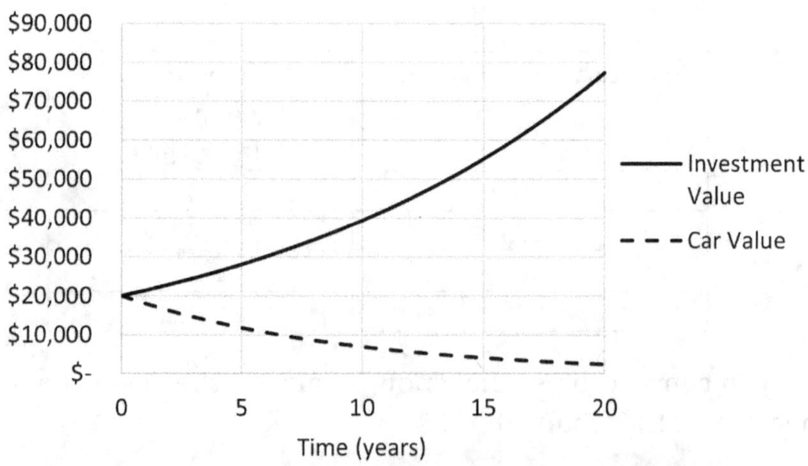

Fig. 3-3 Depreciating vs. Appreciating Asset Value

Usually it's not just as simple as saying, "don't buy it." We need food, clothing, communications, transportation...But the math is the same. If instead of the $40k luxury vehicle you buy the $20k economy car and invest $20k, you've allocated what you can for your future $80k benefit.

These examples illustrate the concept of **opportunity cost**. That means as it sounds: it's the cost to your future net worth not just from the decision today about how to use money, but also the relative under-performance compared to a better opportunity. The concept is that there is always an opportunity to put your resources to work, and the more of your resources you put to work, the better.

From the previous example, consider the purchase of a neutral asset which costs $20,000 and is expected to hold its value – maybe a pile of gold. In comparison, perhaps a near-zero risk-appreciating asset like a bank certificate of deposit or a high yield savings account could grow that $20,000 into $30,000 over some amount of time. Doing something other than taking advantage of the growth available is like paying for that missed opportunity. Over long periods, holding assets like cash can represent a significant drag to your net worth in comparison to putting your money to work for you.

So in general, the recipe for a healthy future balance sheet and maximum personal net wealth is simply a matter of minimizing the amount of your resources going into liabilities or depreciating assets and maximizing the amount going into exponentially appreciating assets.

CHAPTER 4: LET'S GO TO COLLEGE

Before we get ahead of ourselves and forbid any spending, maybe let's get a little perspective.

The biggest example of opportunity cost is possibly the decision to forego earned income and pay for, or take on personal debt to pay for, four years of college. From a quality of life decision, this can be an incredibly complex decision in terms of finding a way to make a living doing what you enjoy, deciding the right college to attend, etc. But let's revisit the example from Chapter 1 and use these concepts of compounding growth to try to answer the question of whether college is a positive financial decision.

We had two options: take a job at $40,000 per year or attend college at a cost of $30,000 per year. Let's assume this is a four year program, and upon graduation you expect to be able to earn $60,000 per year. Consider three scenarios:

-   No College: You decide to go to work at a $40,000 per year job. Your salary will grow at 3% per year, and you'll diligently invest 10% of your salary into an account earning 7% yearly returns.

-   College: You attend college for 4 years incurring $120,000 in student loans (let's assume 0% interest on that – thanks Uncle Sam!). Then you begin work at $60,000 per year; 50% better than without the degree. You save 10% of your salary to first pay off the loans and then pile it into an account earning 7%.

-   College, High Saver: You recognize that you have

extra disposable income due to your high salary, so you use everything you earn in excess of what you'd have with the No College salary to pay off the loans and invest.

The results of this example are in Fig. 4-1. Both College scenarios have you digging a financial hole of $120,000 for the first 4 years, while your Non-College self manages to have around $20,000 invested. From there, if you only save and invest 10% of your salary on the College path, even though you earn more, your net worth is forever higher on the No College path. But, if you recognize that you can live below your means and save more than 10% of your higher salary in the College High Saver path, you can accelerate your net worth to be more than double after 30 years.

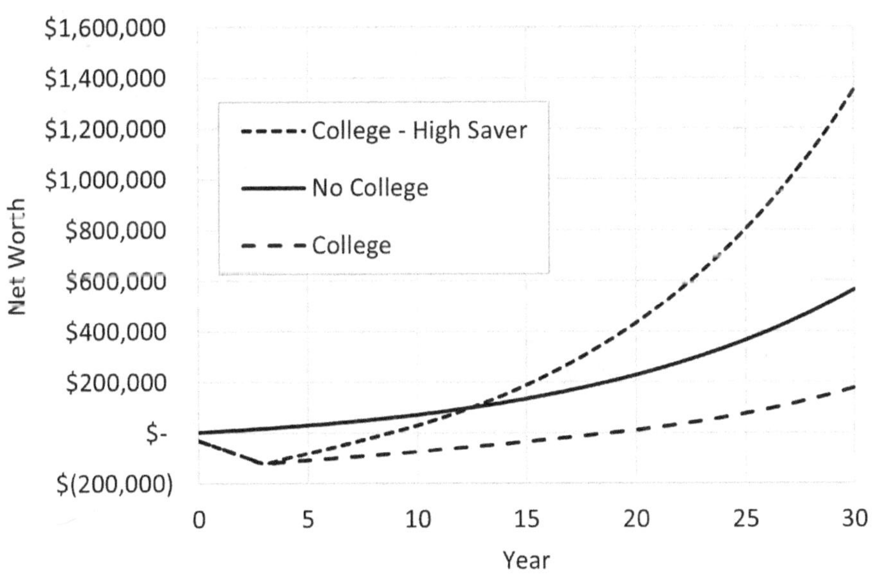

Fig. 4-1 Education Effect on Your Net Worth

Let's consider an alternate universe in which you get into your dream Ivy League school. The bad news: it's $60,000 per year instead of $30,000. Also bad news: your passion of Basket Weaving will only earn you $60,000 after graduation; still 50% more than no degree, but not more than boring Accounting from that far less prestigious college. So what's the effect on your financial future?

Well, as you can see in Fig. 4-2, that $240,000 student loan is quite the anchor on your net worth If you don't set aside more than 10% of your salary, you'll still be broke after 30 years! If you are as diligent as you would have been in the prior High Saver example, you can still eventually make that Basket Weaving degree financially advantageous, but your net worth of $900,000 might be a little disappointing compared to the nearly $1,400,000 as an Accountant from a less prestigious college.

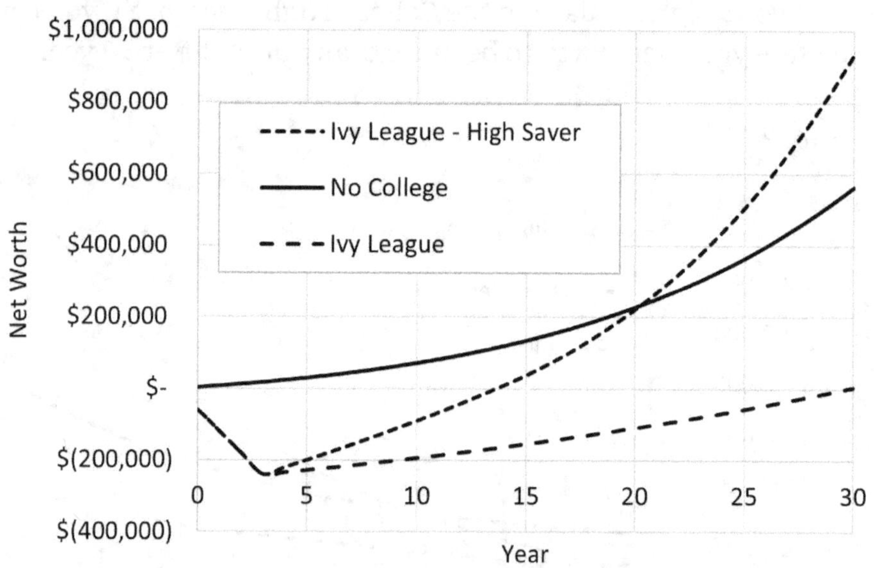

Fig. 4-2 Expensive Education Effect on Your Net Worth

These examples illustrate that concept of opportunity cost; in this case the literal cost of paying tuition vs. not. Generally, if you can afford college at a practical cost and acquire the knowledge and skills for a high-paying career, you will be far better off financially *if you also retain a savings mindset.* Don't take on huge loans and high interest credit card bills to support a fancy lifestyle while you take on debt for tuition!

And they also illustrate the importance of wise financial decisions in your early years. Paying off those loans and beginning to invest as soon as possible will supercharge your wealth later, just like you'd expect from exponential growth.

CHAPTER 5: STOCKS AND BONDS

Ok, you're convinced. You've made your decisions about educating yourself, you're gainfully employed, and you've worked out your budget to avoid fruitless spending and maximize investing. You want to start to invest in your financial future as soon as possible, while you're young. But invest in what?

All investments work by the same general logic of deferred consumption, or delayed gratification. We are willing to set aside some money today in exchange for more money in the future.

The mechanism by which the value grows can vary, but it's always the result of increases in income, or at least the expectations of those increases. The simplest mechanism is by accruing interest by lending the money to someone else in exchange for an agreement to receive more money back in the future. You can do this by depositing your money in a bank savings account, purchasing a certificate of deposit (CD), or buying a government bond that pays a fixed interest rate.

A similar mechanism occurs when you own shares in a company (stock), where you have rights to the company's profits but no agreed-upon fixed rate of interest payment on your investment.

Stocks

So what are stocks, and what gives them "fundamental" value? Isn't this just gambling? ...Definitely not.

Simply put, owning one share of stock in a company is owning the rights to one share of the earnings of that company now and in the future. You literally are part owner of the company, and all of the employees and management team work for you. Earnings of a company are reported on Income Statements on a typically quarterly basis, and similar to our personal income statements, these earnings represent the change in company net worth over the reporting period. A portion of the earnings is typically kept within the company's accounts for investing or other purposes, but a portion is often paid to the shareholders directly in the form of **dividends**.

As an example, let's say you own 1 share in a company for which there are 1,000,000 shares owned by investors out in the world. If that company earns $1M in a year, your share of earnings would be $1...the earnings per share (**EPS**) is $1. But you won't necessarily see that cash come your way. Nor should you necessarily want to. Perhaps the company retains some earnings for building new factories, hiring new experts, or making other strategic acquisitions that it thinks will help it earn even more in the future. So maybe it only sends you $0.50 in dividends. The ratio of the dividend to the price is called the **dividend yield**. In this example, if the price of the stock is $10 per share and the dividend is $0.50 (per year), then the stock is paying a dividend yield of 5%. Most companies will have a dividend yield less than that.

One quick note: dividends are not legally binding. The company may or may not decide to actually pay its expected dividend, and if it makes no profits it may not be able to. So buying stock in a company with a current dividend yield of 20% is not a guarantee of 20% return on your investment...you might be buying stock in a company that people are expecting to go out of business!

Very often, small and growing companies will not pay any dividends at all. When investors have provided capital to grow the company, there is no reason to send money back to the investors.

This is typical practice for high growth tech companies, for example. Stock in companies like that are often called "Growth" stocks.

On the other hand, large and established companies might pay larger dividends if there is not a strong prospect for growing the business further with more investment. Why invest in more factories and machines if we aren't going to sell any more stuff next year? So these companies will send the cash back to the shareholders. This is typical for lower tech industrial companies like railroads or consumer staple producers with stable but slower growing or more stagnant businesses. Stock in companies like this are often called "Value" stocks.

So...what is a share in a company with $1 EPS worth? How much would you pay to buy it? Would you pay more if you knew that next year the company would earn $2, and then $4 the year after? What if the company would be out of business in 5 years? What if it is still developing and won't earn a profit for a few more years?

It is sometimes helpful to think of the price of a stock in terms of the **price to earnings ratio**, or **P/E multiple**; this is simply the per-share stock price divided by the per-share earnings. Investors will tolerate higher P/E multiples for stocks with highly confident and large earnings growth expectations. In fact, a startup company with earnings of $0 has an infinite P/E while it ramps up to become profitable. A successfully fast-growing, market-dominating company with prospects of lasting growth can see its shares priced at P/E levels over 50, 100, or more. This happens when the market expects the future "E" to be far greater than the current "E."

P/E ratios typically will be lower if the growth prospects of a company are lower. If a company is expected to survive but not grow at all, the P/E can be in the single digits. This is often the case for the large industrial companies which pay out a large portion of their earnings as dividends. Over time, the P/E of a stock or group of stocks for similar companies will tend to stay in a somewhat narrow range. For example, the stocks of Ford, GM, Honda, and Toyota all will have similar P/E, but they will likely be very different than the P/E of a small technology startup company's stock.

So, Growth stocks might tend to have high P/E, and Value stocks might tend to have low P/E. But they both carry their own risks. A Growth stock might be a company which never actually reaches expectations and eventually flounders and fails, or maybe never grows to be quite as big as investors hope. This was the case for a lot of the "dot com" companies in the late 1990s. A Value stock could be a company with an old our outdated business model limping along toward its ultimate failure. Think Toys 'R' Us or Sears in the years after Amazon's widespread adoption, or Blockbuster in a world with Netflix.

If you can predict the future earning stream, then you can calculate the "fundamental" value of a stock, which turns out to be the **net present value** of all of the company's future earnings. Net present value attempts to account for the fact that $10 in the future is worth less than $10 today, and then represents the value of all future earnings as a single equivalent lump sum as of today. It accounts for the time-value of money. The first reason for this time-value of money is inflation. If inflation is 5% per year, then earnings of $10.50 given to you in a year will be worth the same as $10 given to you today. So using 5% as the **discount rate**, the net present value of $10.50 one year from now is $10.

The second reason is that concept of opportunity cost; if I can invest $10 today and have it grow over time with little risk, it will be worth more than $10. If the bank will pay me 10% interest on a risk-free deposit, then I can grow $10 today into $11.00 in a year.

Calculating the net present value of even a *known* stream of incomes in the future can get complicated due to different adjustments for rates and opportunity costs. Calculating the net present value of the *unknown* stream of incomes in the future associated with a company's earnings is even more uncertain. If investors forecast that a company will grow fast, then they will be willing to buy the stock at a higher P/E multiple. But buyer beware: those future earnings are uncertain!

This uncertainty is the source of volatility in stock prices. If war breaks out somewhere in the world, shareholders of US stocks might predict tougher economic times and hence reduced corporate profits, sending the market value of stocks lower. Stock traders will collectively attempt to forecast the future's effect on the net present value of the company's earnings to determine the amount that they'd pay to own (or sell) the stock. But over the long run, as the actual earnings come in, the truth reveals itself and the stock price will tend to settle on that reasonable P/E range.

But owning companies is the allure of owning stocks. If you invested early in Amazon, Google, Netflix, Nvidia, Starbucks, or Tesla, before they had billions in earnings, you eventually saw tremendous returns on your investment. But, if you invested in Pets.com or Enron, you saw your investment eventually evaporate with the businesses themselves. This is why we diversify (more on this in the next Chapter).

Bonds

Compared to stocks, bonds are more predictable because they involve a loan and contract to repay that loan with interest. When you buy a bond, you essentially loan money to the bond issuer. Maybe a municipality needs to borrow money to build a water treatment plant, or a company needs to borrow money to fund some capital improvements. They "sell" bonds as a way to acquire cash they need now and will pay back later. The bond is something you buy in exchange for a promise to receive your money back at a future date, plus interest.

For example, a company might issue 5-year bonds at 6% interest. If you bought a $10 **face value** bond, you would be paid $.60 per year for 5 years, and then receive your $10 back after the 5 years is over. If the company's earnings grow tremendously, you still only get 6% interest. If the company makes no earnings at all, they still owe you that 6% interest.

In the rare circumstance that a company goes bankrupt, the bond holders have priority over the stock shareholders in terms of who gets paid. So the bankrupt company might sell all of its assets, pay the bond holders with the proceeds, and if there's nothing left for the stock shareholders then it's tough cookies for them!

Typically bonds are more stable than stocks, with more reliable non-negative returns, but with lesser long term growth potential.

If you hold a bond until **maturity**, when the bond issuer pays back your principal, you will receive your principal back and have investment growth according to the bond's rate. However, you may choose to sell the bond to someone else before the term is up. Similarly, you might wish to buy a bond that someone previously bought before it matures. It turns out that there is a market for bonds just like there is for stocks, and so they need not be held to maturity. But, because of the effect of market interest rates, the value of your bonds can go down (or up).

Here's why. Let's say you buy a "zero coupon" bond for $98 with a face value of $100, due in 2 years. This means you loaned $98 today in exchange for $100 in 2 years, and no interest in the form of "coupons" is paid in the meantime. This bond is paying a low **yield**, or interest rate, paying you only $2 (around 1% APR) over the term. Now, imagine that the US government, the most reliable borrower in the world with the power of taxation so they should never default, issues 2-year bonds at a 5% interest rate. The market value for a reliable, stable 2-year $100 face value bond has then been established at around $91 (since $91 earning 5% per year for 2 years will be $100). If you try to sell *your* 2 year bond to someone else on the open market, they wouldn't pay you $98... they would maybe pay you $91 at best. So, you'll lose $7 on your $98 investment if you choose to sell.

In contrast, imagine you paid $91 for that $100 face value bond originally, and now the US government is issuing bonds at a 1% rate, meaning they will take around $98 today in exchange for paying back $100 in 2 years. Well, the value of the bond you hold will now be closer to $98, and so you could sell for a faster gain on your investment than the original interest yield.

So bond holders will tend to see the value of their bonds increase in times when interest rates are decreasing, and decrease in times when interest rates are increasing. But the magnitude and speed of the changes in value is typically far smaller than the magnitude and speed of changes in stock prices, and if the bonds are held to maturity then the rate of return reflects the interest rate at the time of purchase.

For this reason, the financial advice will sometimes be to own a blend of stocks and bonds to balance the goals of minimizing short-term risk while seeking long-term returns. As your investment horizon gets shorter, conventional wisdom says that the proportion of bonds in your portfolio would go up to minimize the short-term risk associated with stocks. This is the situation as you get older or if you have near-term needs for the funds.

CHAPTER 6: DIVERSIFICATION AND MANAGING INVESTMENT RISK

We covered the importance of investing in appreciating assets like stocks, because in contrast to neutral assets or even bonds, their rate of return can be higher. And we don't want to miss out on that opportunity to compound at a high rate for decades!

But, we also saw how a stock can become worthless if the underlying company's business fails. And in the very short term, stock prices reflect news and rumors and can be volatile. And, the stock's dividend yield, unlike the bond's interest, is not a contractual obligation owed to the stock holder and might not even be paid. So doesn't that all mean that stocks are risky?

Well yes, absolutely. And in some sense that is why the potential rate of return is higher, because not everyone is willing to take that risk all the time and buy stocks. The fluctuation in stock value in the short term can be very volatile. A rumor on the internet, an off-hand comment from the CEO, a positive or negative review by an influencer on social media...although extremely rare, an individual stock's daily price can swing by 50% or more on the right or wrong news. *In the short term.*

But there are two ways to combat a stock's short-term price volatility and long term business risk: Time and Diversification.

Minimizing Risk with Time

In the short term, a stock's price can be volatile. But in the long term, because a stock is the right to a stream of earnings, the price of the stock will tend to follow the company's earnings such that a "normal" P/E multiple should exist. Today's good news will be offset by next week's bad news, and perhaps in 2 years the daily blips will be long forgotten.

Consider a stock in Coca-Cola, and imagine in 1990 the P/E multiple was 10. Fast forward to 2020. Is the business fundamentally different? No, not really. So what P/E would investors be willing to pay? 8? 12? Certainly not 50. So how can the stock price be any higher than it was in 1990? Simple: if the E is bigger, the P will be proportionally bigger as well. So the price will track the earnings.

Let's look at the price of Apple (with stock symbol AAPL) over the course of part of 2023 in Fig. 6-1. Data on publicly traded companies like this is available on Yahoo Finance or Google Finance or many other websites. Over this time period, there is some substantial volatility, including big changes between the income reports in August and November. Why? Who knows?! Buying and selling during this period would be risky unless you literally could forecast the short term future and how the swarm of investors will trade shares among themselves and react to various tidbits of news.

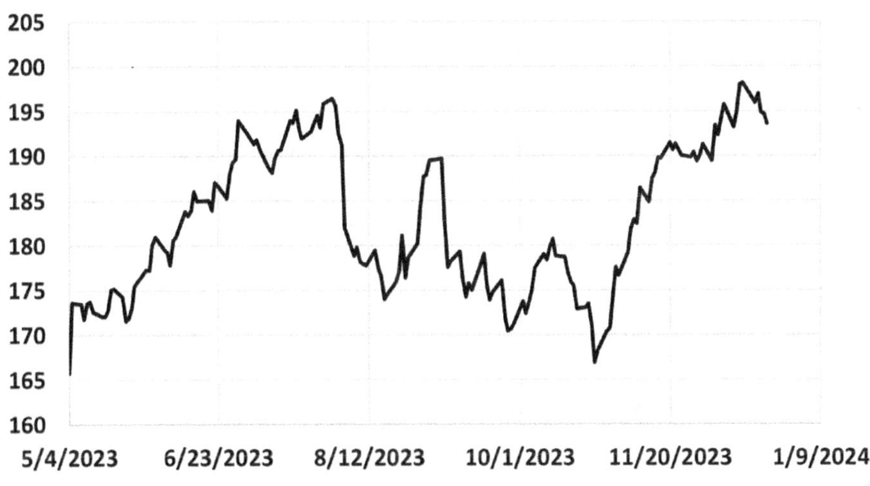

Fig. 6-1 AAPL Share Price in 2023

If we zoom out and look at the 5 year timeframe in Fig. 6-2, the story is a bit different. Among the short-term volatility is a steady upward climb reflecting the company's growing earnings. The massive stock market shock in early 2020 associated with the COVID-19 pandemic is long forgotten by 2023. In fact, remember what the stock is: rights to *future* earnings. What happened in the past is of zero consequence. And in the long run the company's stock is staying within a range of P/E...the P is tracking the E.

Fig. 6-2 AAPL Share Price from 2019 to 2024

The tendency of stocks to have prices that track their earnings in the long run, and to suffer short-term volatility all the while, is what gives rise to the "buy and hold" philosophy. Very few people short of (illegal) insider traders can forecast the short-term volatility with any accuracy. Short-term stock trading is in some sense a zero-sum gain. There is a reason why it's called **trading** rather than investing. The price is reflective of the buying and selling price among active market transactions. For every person netting a 10% short-term gain on AAPL in September of 2023, there is a person netting a 10% short-term loss. Almost nobody has success more than half the time trying to time or predict the short-term volatility.

On the other hand, everybody has success in the long run, where the real economic gains that a company makes are reflected in their increased earnings and consequentially higher stock value. Remember, when you own the stock, you own the rights to the profits, and all of the employees are working for you. All of that innovation and marketing and sales that Apple did from 2019-2023 is to your benefit as long as you own the stock over that period.

If you are a young investor making regular investments as you earn income, you will inadvertently smooth out this volatility without even trying. It's called **dollar cost averaging**. Take a look again at that AAPL plot in 2023, and imagine you're investing $100 every 2 weeks when you get paid. Looking back, you might think you overpaid in July, but you also bought the stock when it was cheap in late October! In October, your $100 was able to purchase more shares. So over time, by regularly investing, you will smooth out that short term volatility and capture the long-term growth.

This is why highly regarded investors like Warren Buffett will often explain how the money to be made in investing is not by "buying low and selling high." It's from buying stock in the right companies and waiting while they grow their businesses on your behalf!

Minimizing Risk with Diversification

Even when owning a stock for a long time to smooth out the short term market swings, there is a possibility that the underlying business will fail or fall short of expectations. The old expression about the eggs and the basket applies. Even a small probability of your investment hitting $0 is unacceptably high risk, so you probably don't want all your money in Apple stock, even if it has performed pretty well.

The way to avoid this risk is to diversify among companies, industries, and countries by owning a broad swath of stocks. The probability of *every* company having its stock price go to zero is tiny. And in the event that does happen...well, the amount of canned food in your doomsday bunker is probably a bigger concern.

Studies have generally shown that a diverse group of 20-50 stocks is a large enough cross-section to achieve "full diversification." But the good news is that people have been thinking about this and looking at this for a while, so you can do even better, and it's extremely easy.

Diversification is usually easiest achieved through **Mutual Funds**. Mutual funds are groups of stocks held in some mix and proportion by an institution such that when you buy a share of the mutual fund, you own that blend of stocks. They are convenient for quickly and easily using your $400 monthly investment to achieve a broadly diversified coverage of stocks in a single transaction.

Mutual funds generally come in two varieties: Actively managed funds and passive index funds.

Actively managed funds involve a fund manager who has the job of allocating your money to the right blend and proportion of stocks. They might set up the fund to focus on technology, or finance, or agriculture, or only European stocks, whatever. Then they charge you a fee every year to manage the fund, typically around 2% of the investment's value. The claim is that these investment managers are smarter than you, so you should pay them 2% of your wealth every year to allocate your investments smartly.

The problem with actively managed funds is this: remember the zero-sum short-term trading example? It turns out that for every over-performing fund manager, there is an under-performing fund manager. None of them actually can predict the future. And studies have shown that past performance of a fund manager does not reliably predict future performance. So what we have is an industry of fund managers playing a zero-sum short-term trading game with everyone else's money. On average, they are no better than "the market." But guess what? They all are taking 2% per year of their customers' wealth regardless!

John Bogle founded the financial investment firm Vanguard after researching this problem and identifying the disservice to personal investors resulting from actively managed fund fees.

The solution: extremely low cost funds which simply aggregate stocks according to an index representing the diversified market. If all the active managers will compare themselves to the index anyway, and for every good manager there is a bad one, why not just own the blend in the index and skip the 2% fee?

The low cost index fund has been a huge benefit for individual investors by making the investment world accessible to everyone without that 2% fee. Here's why. Remember our roadmap to being a millionaire by 60 by investing $3,000 up front and $400 a month and seeing 7% return on our investment? Well, a 2% fund management fee means a 5% return every year, not 7%. You think that doesn't sound too bad? Well, rather than your stock portfolio reaching $1,003,172 by age 60, it only reaches $600,959, around 40% less! That's right...that active management didn't just cost you a measly 2%, it compounded every year to cost you $400,000 in wealth!

Low cost index funds are available with fees in the 0.1% range (or less) covering many indices. The Dow Jones Industrial Average (DJIA) is an index of large US industrial companies. The Standard and Poor's (S&P) 500 is an index of 500 US companies covering technology, health care, agriculture, construction...everything. And it is periodically updated to ensure that the companies in the index are well run and stable. Then there's the NASDAQ 100 (100 leading technology companies), the Russell 2000 ("small" companies). There are international indices tracking European or Asian markets. You get the idea.

The S&P 500 has become the de facto standard for index investing, and for good reason. It gives you access to the entire US economy including many companies with significant global market participation. Companies including Apple, but companies in other industries including financial, energy, food, agriculture, technology, medical, retail, transportation...

The value of the S&P 500 index over the past several decades is shown in Fig. 6-3. While individual companies in the index could fail, the index at large will not because it is broadly diversified and spans the whole US economy. And the long-term Price tracks the Earnings, as it should. When you own the S&P 500, all those companies are working for you. Every time someone buys a box of Cheerios or an iPhone or some Nike shoes, or fills a prescription at Walgreens, or buys a new house mortgaged by Bank of America, a tiny slice of profit comes your way. Waiting in line at Starbucks, rather than worrying about how long the line is, you're thinking, "boy, I bet same-store sales are really up this year...that's great for my investments!"

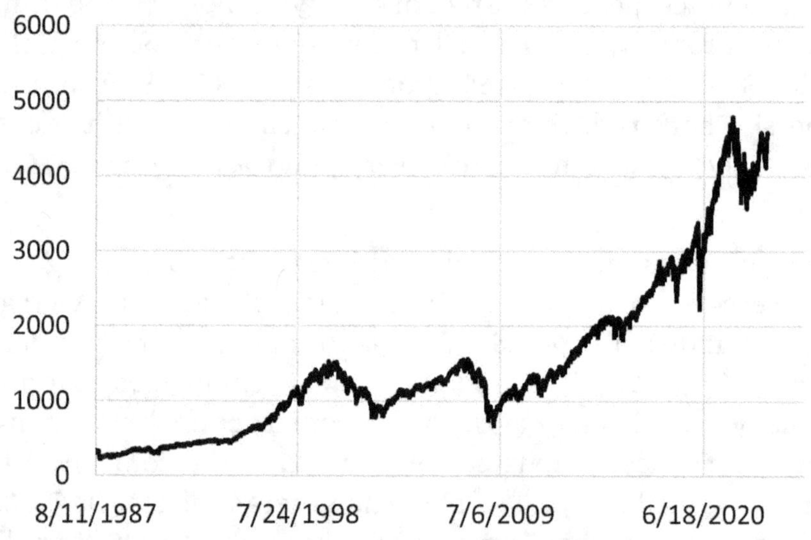

Fig. 6-3 S&P 500 Index Price

Temporary volatility still exists and can be significant. You can see the late-1990s "dot-com" bubble (and subsequent burst). But things recovered, because that was a period when the P/E was too high because stock traders were too optimistic about growth, and eventually reality set in when the actual earnings weren't as high as the optimism had hoped. There's the 2008 financial crisis crash, followed by the strong 2010's recovery. The COVID-19 pandemic caused a crash in 2020, followed by a fast recovery and bubble in 2021, which corrected in 2022. Some blips up, some blips down, everything tracking the broader US economy and the sum of all corporate earnings. If you're dollar-cost averaging, over time it's almost irrelevant.

Something else, barely visible on this plot: "Black Monday," the crash of 1987, where the DJIA index fell 22.6% and the S&P 500 dropped 25% in a single day. At the time, traumatic. In this plot, a barely visible blip. Because whether you were dollar-cost averaging and bought shares the day before or the day after that crash in 1987, by 2007 you saw huge returns.

So let's revisit the discussion of exponential growth and US GDP. How does the S&P 500 compare? Is that 7% per year exponential growth we used in previous investment examples realistic? The plots below show the S&P 500 price (value) from 1972 to 2023, around 50 years of history. The plot on the top is curving up and the logarithmic plot on the bottom is close to a straight line. Looks exponential!

Fig. 6-4 S&P 500 Price from 1972 to 2023

If you fit an exponential curve to each decade, you find that the S&P 500 price does indeed follow the exponential growth trend, shown in Fig. 6-5. Aside from the 1970s, a period notorious for a stagnant economy, persistent inflation, and the global oil supply crisis, in which the S&P 500 trend is about 2% growth per year, the remaining data trends on a growth rate around 8% per year. Of course there are ups and downs, but this sure looks a lot like the 6.5% long term growth we saw from the greater US GDP.

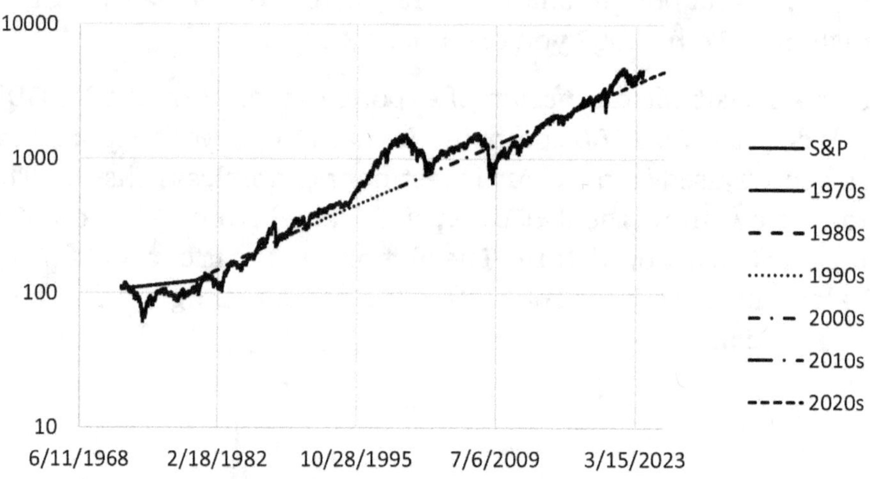

Fig. 6-5 S&P 500 Price with Exponential Fits

It's important to again remember why this is the case. In contrast to a bar of gold or some bitcoin stored on your hard drive, this growth in value is the result of actual work and innovation across the broader economy. There is rationality in expecting exponential growth from investments in these companies.

In previous sections we showed the importance of investing early in your life to benefit from years of compounding exponential growth. Here, we've shown the importance of having a long-term investment horizon and a broadly diverse portfolio of stocks for the purpose of minimizing risk associated with short-term market fluctuations or single-company events and for ensuring that we capture the overall growth of the US economy.

And, we've explained how best to do that: low cost, passive index funds.

So how do you get started? If you have a long investment horizon, do what you can to scrape together an initial investment. Go to vanguard.com or fidelity.com and look into opening an account. Buy shares in VFINX (Vanguard's S&P 500 index fund with 0.14% expense ratio). Or FXAIX: Fidelity's S&P 500 index fund with a 0.02% expense ratio and no minimum initial investment. Or even FZROX, Fidelity's total stock market index fund, which is even broader than the S&P 500. And then remember the long term vision, and stay disciplined with your investing by making regular investments to dollar-cost average.

What about bonds? Over the very long run, a diversified blend of stocks will reap better rewards. But even that diversified blend can lose value in short periods. And "short" could be years; take a look again at the late 1990s and after the 2008 crash. If you expect to need your money to spend in the next year or two, and can't afford so see a drop in value, consider holding cash or bonds (low cost diversified bond index funds are also available). This also becomes a concern in your later years, near retirement, since you will likely be using your investments to provide income. But if you're in your 20s, you have decades before you should consider passing on the opportunity that owning stocks offers.

You will need to decide about what type of account you do your investing in, since it will affect your taxes and access to your investment. We'll cover that next...

CHAPTER 7: TAXES AND TYPES OF INVESTMENT ACCOUNTS

Taxes muddy the investment decision choices significantly and give rise to the huge industry of financial advisors, tax attorneys, and estate planners. The tax environment will influence where you decide to keep your investments for the purpose of reducing your tax burden. Let's try to simplify it.

First, let's look at the income tax code. Here in the US we have a system that tends to lessen the tax burden for folks with lower incomes (not lower net worth, an important distinction).

The first way this is done is through a system of **deductions**. The first step in determining how much income tax you owe is determining your taxable income:

Taxable income = Gross income – deductions

Deductions can be itemized for things like mortgage interest, charitable donations, childcare costs, and other things. But the Internal Revenue Service (IRS) sets a **standard deduction** every year which can be used for simplicity to determine your taxable income. The standard deduction in 2023 for an individual is $13,850. This means that if you earn less than $13,850 per year, your taxable income is less than zero after crediting the standard deduction and you will owe no federal income tax.

The second way the tax burden is lessened for lower incomes is through a graduated income tax structure. As you earn more money, you'll pay an increasing amount of tax on that income. This is done through **tax brackets**, where the portion of money you earn above certain thresholds is taxed at an increasing amount. For 2023 the tax brackets giving the tax rate applied to your taxable income is:

- $0 to $11,000:   10%
- to $44,725:   12%
- to $95,375:   22%
- to $182,100:   24%
- to $231,250:   32%
- to $578,125:   35%
- over $578,125:   37%

If you earn $75,000 in a year (taxable income), this does not mean that *you* are taxed at 22%. This means that *your income* from below $11,000 is taxed at 10% ($1,100), *your income* from $11,000 to $44,725 is taxed at 12% ($5,147), and then *your income* from $44,725 to $75,000 is taxed at 22% ($6,661), so your total tax liability is $11,807.

The amount of income tax you will owe as a function of your original gross income is shown in Fig. 7-1. The line steepens as your income grows, especially in going from the 12% to 22% rate starting at $58,575 on a gross basis.

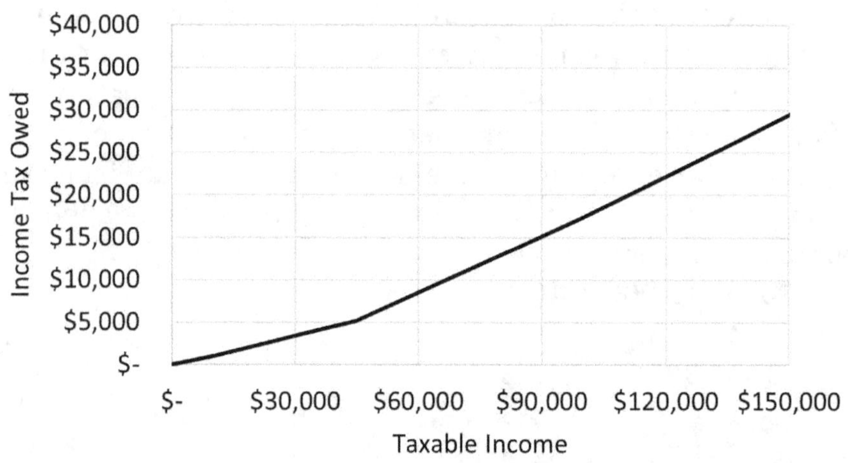

Fig. 7-1 Income Tax vs. Taxable Income (2023)

The different types of investment accounts are all different strategies to minimize your tax burden.

Personal Accounts

A personal taxable account offers nothing special with respect to income tax strategies. Earnings from the sale of investments (you buy a stock for $50 and then sell it some years later for $100) are subject to **capital gains** tax, typically ranging (currently) up to 15%. If the gain is "short term," meaning you owned the asset for less than a year, the earning is taxed as normal income. Dividends from stocks and interest payments on bonds or savings accounts are also taxed as income.

Personal accounts for stocks, bonds, mutual funds, and other investments are held by institutions such as Vanguard, Fidelity, Charles Schwab, and others. They all will have nice websites and smartphone and tablet apps, easy links to/from your bank's checking account, options for automatically recurring investments, etc.

Institutions such as Vanguard and Fidelity offer their own mutual fund products, such as the S&P 500 index fund options we mentioned previously. You can initiate an account simply by purchasing shares in such funds. Or, you can create a "brokerage" fund, where the company acts as a broker on your behalf such that you can buy and sell assets on the open market beyond just the company's offerings, including individual stocks.

401(k) and 403(b) Accounts

401(k) and 403(b) accounts are employer-sponsored accounts for corporations and government entities, respectively. These accounts have tax advantages in that the contributions you make into the accounts are deductions from your gross income. The investments can grow tax-free for the ensuing years until you reach retirement; you do not pay capital gains or income taxes on investments or their dividends within these accounts. Then, when you take **distributions** from the account (withdraw money), it is taxed as income. These accounts are often referred to as being "tax deferred." These accounts will be maintained by companies acting on behalf of the employer.

The catch here is that 401(k) and 403(b) accounts are intended to be retirement accounts, and you cannot withdraw funds from the account without a penalty until age 59 ½. After age 72, you are required to withdraw a minimum amount every year according to your age. So if you want to invest your money so you can buy your Cadillac at age 50, 401(k) and 403(b) accounts are not designed for that.

These accounts typically have limited investment options. To keep program costs down, perhaps only a handful of stock and bond mutual funds will be offered. There are brokerage funds, however, within which your investment options would be broad. But typically a few low cost index funds are available.

One major advantage of these accounts is the concept of the **employer match**. Usually an employer will help you contribute to your fund by matching some amount of your contributions.

For example, maybe they'll match 50% of your contributions up to some fraction of your pay, maybe 8% or 10%. So if you put 8% of your salary into the investment account, your employer would put in an additional 4%. If your employer offers this, you absolutely *must* take advantage of it fully! It's like a 4% or 5% pay raise, put into a tax-protected lock box for compounding!

Because of the tax benefits, the US government puts a cap on its generosity. Contributions to 401(k) and 403(b) accounts are limited to $22,500 per year (in 2023 – the limit is constantly adjusted upward with inflation).

Pensions

50 years ago, people would go to work for an employer, stay there for a career, and retire knowing that they could rely on a steady monthly pension to fund their golden years. Not any more. The trend among private industry employers outside of government (teachers, police, government employees) is to eliminate and never speak again of pension programs. This is mostly in response to the rise of the 401(k) and 403(b) options and to address the fact that a more dynamic and mobile workforce is less interested in hands-off assurances of payments 40 years down the line.

That said, if you are lucky enough to have access to a pension program, consider using it as a supplement to your own saving. If you need to choose between 401(k) / 403(b) options or participation in the pension program, you'll need to consider the possible difference in benefit to you.

If you're truly a long way from retirement, which is the case if you're in your 20s, pension programs usually have less immediate and clear benefit. The reason is because they typically are structured along the lines of contributing some amount of your pay now for some amount of regular pay in perpetuity after retirement. So maybe you contribute 2% of your salary for the same amount of dollars every year after age 65.

Whereas setting aside 2% of your pay at age 64 to receive that same amount back every year after retirement is an obviously good deal, setting aside 2% of your pay when you're 25 and missing out on 40 years of compounding investment growth (and watching that dollar amount effectively shrink due to inflation) might not be.

Another possible downside of pension programs is the lack of control. You trust the employer or pension fund manager to wisely monitor and invest the funds such that it remains funded when you come along to collect. There are historical examples of pension fund mismanagement, however, where expecting retirees see reduced or lost pension payments.

We discussed in Chapter 5 how you can reduce risk in your stock portfolio through diversification and with a long-term investment outlook. Participation in pension funds should be viewed as valuable supplemental diversification to your own investing. If you need to choose between 401(k)/403(b) participation or a pension, do the math and determine if the offered pension is competitive with what you can expect from your own investing. If the pension is available as a supplement, consider participating to additionally reduce risk associated with your own investment portfolio.

Individual Retirement Accounts

Individual Retirement Accounts (IRAs) are similar to 401(k) and 403(b) accounts, except that you initiate and maintain them personally. They are also "tax deferred," and contributions can be credited as deductions from your gross income for income tax purposes. Typically the same firms that offer personal accounts (Vanguard, Fidelity, etc.) will also offer IRA accounts.

IRA contributions in 2023 are limited to $6,500 per year, or your taxable income, whichever is lower. If you have no income, you cannot contribute to an IRA. But, even if you have access to a 401(k) or 403(b) through your employer, you can still have and invest in your own IRA up to the limit.

Also like 401(k) and 403(b) accounts, withdrawal from the account must occur after age 59 ½ or else you must treat the withdrawal as income and pay a 10% penalty. Considering that you didn't pay income tax on that money to begin with, and perhaps you'd need to pay 10% capital gains tax on a personal account anyway, that's not so severe a penalty such that these accounts should be overlooked.

Roth Accounts

A "Roth" account is named after the legislation creating the concept. These accounts are variants of 401(k), 403(b), and "Traditional" IRA accounts with a slight twist.

In Roth accounts, your contributions are made "after tax," meaning they do not reduce your taxable income in the year the contribution is made. However, because the income tax on the money has already been paid, future distributions are not subject to income tax in the future. While investments in the account grow, they are not subject to any taxes in the same manner as the non-Roth accounts.

So what's the point of a Roth? Consider the tax brackets. Imagine you are currently earning $30k per year and so your highest tax rate is 12%. But you foresee yourself extremely wealthy in the future. When you take a distribution from your account, you'll be in a higher tax bracket, and so you'll pay taxes at a higher rate!

It's as simple as that. If you are going to be in a higher tax bracket in the future, you're better off paying the income tax on the money now and contributing to the Roth account. If you're going to be in a lower bracket, you're better off taking the income deduction on the contribution to the Traditional account now, and paying the income tax on the distribution later. If your tax bracket won't change, then it doesn't matter. If you aren't sure, consider contributing to both types.

Another consideration is the tax rates themselves. If the income tax rates are going up in the future, do a Roth. This is more likely the case than the inverse, as US government debt continues to climb and the current tax rates are low compared to historical averages.

Prioritizing Your Allocations

Ok, so you're young, starting work, beginning your life. You might not have $6500 a year to contribute to an IRA *and* $22,500 a year to contribute to a 401(k) which you won't see until retirement. You might even be thinking about buying a house (we'll cover that in the next section). What should you do? Consider the advantages and disadvantages of each option in the table below.

Account Type	Advantages	Disadvantages	Reasons to Utilize
Personal	• Easy access, easy transfer to bank accounts	• Income tax on dividends and capital gains	• Access to the funds without penalty before retirement • Reached limit on tax-advantaged contributions
401(k) / 403(b)	• Employer match (effective salary increase) • Reduced income tax burden (now) • Tax-deferred growth	• Early withdrawal penalties	• Get full employee benefits through <u>match</u> • Income tax rate now is expected to be higher than in retirement
Traditional IRA	• Reduced income tax burden (now) • Tax-deferred growth	• Early withdrawal penalties	• Income tax rate now is expected to be higher than in retirement
Roth 401(k) / 403(b) / IRA	• Employer match (effective salary increase for 401/403) • Tax-deferred growth	• Early withdrawal penalties • No current income tax benefit	• Income tax rate now is expected to be lower than in retirement

First, if your employer offers a match on 401(k) or 403(b) investments, make sure you contribute the amount needed to maximize their match! If they offer 50% matching up to 8% of your salary, then be sure to contribute 8% of your salary.

Next, people will have different opinions about a "rainy day" fund, but it is nice to try to save at least one or two months' salary in a simple savings account. Set up a personal account at Vanguard or Fidelity. You can establish a high yield or money market savings position and begin to invest in those low cost diversified index funds. If you feel secure in your employment situation, those investments can partly be considered your rainy day fund since they can quickly be sold and money transferred to your checking account.

There is really no rush to establish an IRA; it's more important to just start regular investing. But it will be easy to set up both an IRA and personal account at the same time. As you can, you can try to start putting extra funds into your IRA account. When you're young, a Roth IRA is probably better than a Traditional IRA, since you're likely to be in a higher tax bracket as you get older.

If you can stretch your budget and max out the IRA contribution, then, as you find yourself able, increase your 401(k) or 403(b) contributions beyond the minimum needed for the company match. As you get older you may want to consider a blend of Roth and Traditional approaches, depending on your income expectations and the relative advantages and disadvantages of each approach.

Probably not far into this process, you'll look at your spending and saving and realize a significant chunk of your money is going to rent. Your budget is not entirely going to be allocated to investing! Rent is obviously not an appreciating asset helping your long term wealth...so let's discuss the alternative next.

CHAPTER 8: MORTGAGES AND BUYING A HOUSE

Buying a house can either be financially pretty ok or a complete disaster, depending on the situation. In the US, the common perception is that our home is our largest investment, the key to financial independence and long term wealth. Unfortunately, that is a bit of a stretch. Home ownership can be beneficial as part of your financial portfolio, but as we'll soon see, you'll need to find the right balance between home ownership and other investments.

The reason for exponential growth of appreciating assets is that every year, some incremental gain in productivity, efficiency, innovation, or market size leads to an incremental gain in the underlying asset's earnings. For stocks and bonds, that is either through a percentage interest payment with reinvestment (bonds) or an incremental improvement in corporate earnings (stocks).

What would be the reason for exponential growth of a home's value? It produces the exact same thing now and forever: shelter and square footage. Will it double its utility in 10 years and therefore justify a 7% per year growth rate? No, it will not. For this reason, aside from regional demographic forces, a home tends to be a neutral asset in the long run: retaining its value (assuming it is maintained and located in a habitable/desirable location) relative to currency. So yes, it will grow exponentially, but should generally track the exponential growth of currency inflation. But as can be shown by some examples, home ownership can be used as a supplement to your investments to maximize your long term wealth if used wisely.

Case 1: Buy the House

When you buy a house, unless you pay cash (consider the opportunity cost of that!), you borrow money from a bank in the form of a mortgage. Typically you make a down payment, and then borrow money to cover the rest. Let's say the bank approves your mortgage application to buy a $100,000 house. (Good luck finding a house for that much anywhere, but it's a nice even number that makes illustrating the concepts easy. If you are in the market for a $400,000 house, just multiply everything here by 4. Or if you live in San Francisco, multiply by 10!)

The standard is to pay 20% down and to take on a 30-year loan. On the day of the house purchase, you pay $20k and acquire both a $100k house (asset) and an $80k mortgage (liability). Aside from the lawyer fees, closing costs, taxes, realtor fees, etc., which can be significant and usually range anywhere from 2-9% of the $100k price, there is no change to your net worth. You have 20% **equity** in your house; this is the amount of the house's value which you own in excess of the loan's **principal** (outstanding balance still owed to the bank).

For the next 30 years, you will make a monthly payment. A fraction of that payment will go toward the interest on the outstanding loan. The rest will go toward paying off the principal over the 30 years. You'll also have property tax owed to your local municipality, and homeowner's insurance to protect against catastrophes. This will vary, but let's assume a typical rate of 2% of the property value per year covers both.

The first month you own the house, you need to make a payment. Let's assume the annual percentage rate (APR) is 6%. You can go online to a loan calculator, or use the formula from Chapter 2, and determine that your monthly payment will be $479.64 to pay off the loan. How much will you pay the bank, and how much will you pay yourself by paying off the loan? Well, the first month you'll owe the bank one twelfth of 6% (0.5%) of the principal, $80k, in interest, or $400. You'll pay yourself $79.64 in the form of reducing the size of your mortgage with a payment toward the principal. Oh, and don't forget that $166.67 in property tax and insurance.

So, you're looking at $566.67 in lost money (the interest plus taxes), which you can think of as a rent payment that you pay to the bank and the neighborhood. And you've invested $79.64 into residential real estate. Your net worth increases by that $79.64, which is far smaller than the total monthly payment of $646.31.

Now imagine you're buying a $400,000 house...after coming up with the $80k down payment, your "rent" payment on your $320k mortgage is still $2,267 per month! Something to consider is the cost of actually renting; if you can rent a comparable house for much less than this "rent," then the house might be over-priced for its market.

A key ingredient here is the APR of your mortgage. Like all loans you have, the higher the rate, the worse it is for your net worth. Fig. 8-1 shows how higher rates not only mean that the total monthly payment goes up, but the fraction of your initial payments going toward your principal also goes down. At 8% APR, as you start paying your mortgage payments, over 70% of your money goes to the bank in the form of an interest payment and only 5% stays in your pocket in the form of home equity.

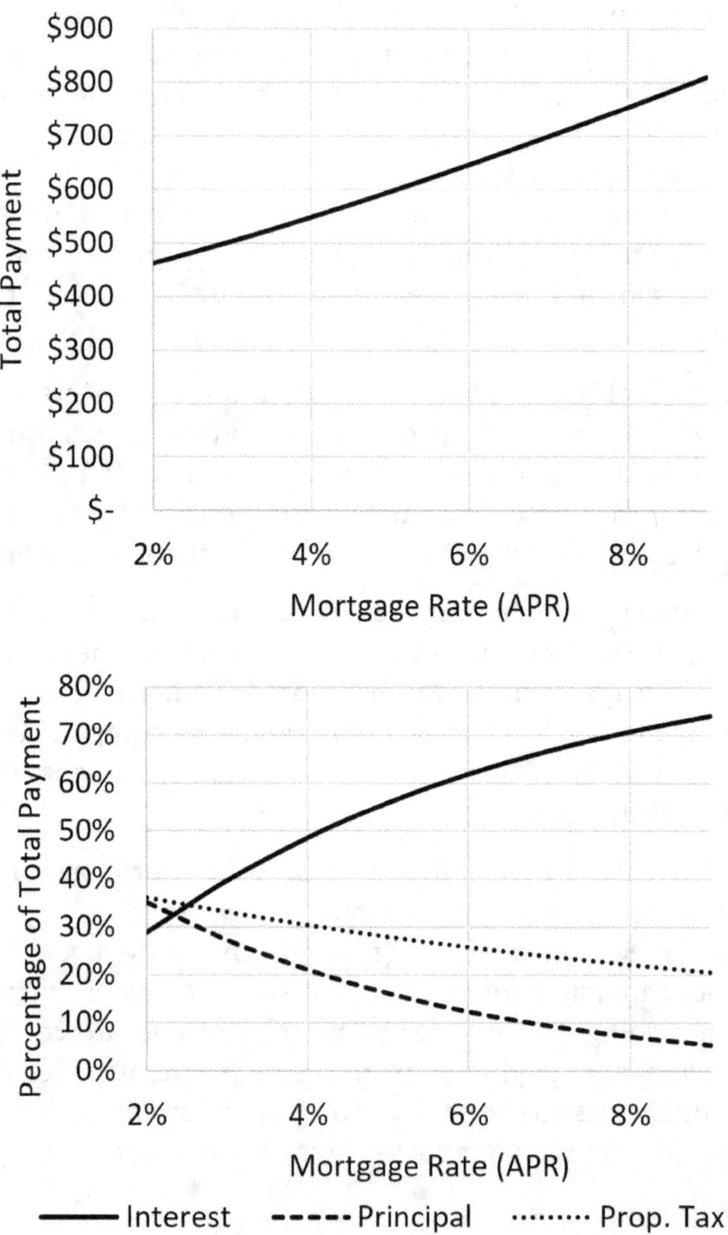

Fig. 8-1 Effect of Mortgage APR on Monthly Payment

It is not all doom and gloom. In subsequent months and years, the situation improves as the loan's principal reduces. Every month you owe less interest on the loan, and so more of your monthly payment goes toward paying down the loan. Back to our example with 6% APR, a little bit before the 20 year mark, you finally start paying yourself as much as you're paying the bank every month. Fig. 8-2 shows the **amortization** of the loan.

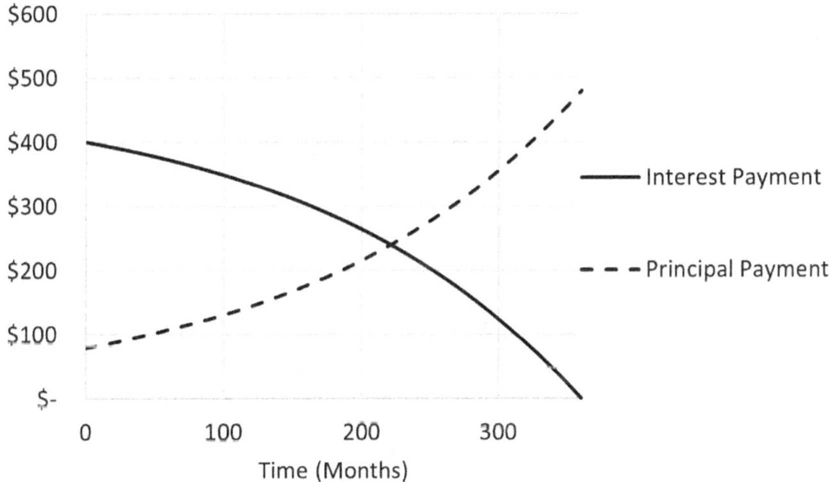

Fig. 8-2 Amortization of 6% APR Loan

Over time, as you chip away at the principal, you own more and more of your own house. And, the value of the house itself will likely appreciate over time, perhaps tracking inflation or even beating inflation depending on the relative strength of the regional economy. So as time goes on, your equity increases just by virtue of the home's value increasing. Let's assume the home value grows at 3% per year over the 30 year loan. How does your net worth change? Well, in this case, shown in Fig. 8-3, your $100k house is eventually worth around $250k. Because of the appreciation, it's worth more than the sum of your payments to the bank! But, including the property tax you pay along the way, it's worth less.

Nonetheless, this is why home ownership can, and does, provide a source of financial stability over time. If you can manage to purchase your own residence for an amount not significantly more than renting, this example shows how over time you can add to your net worth.

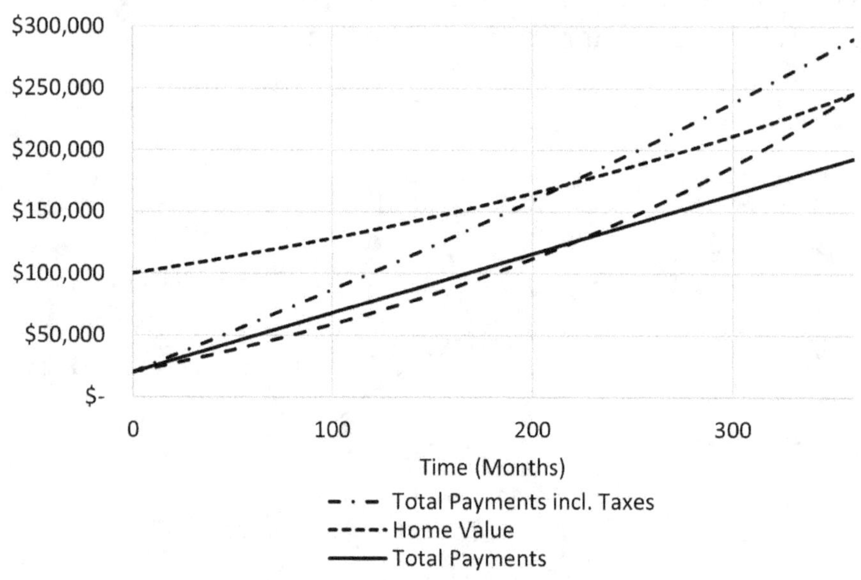

Fig. 8-3 Case 1 Home Purchase Scenario

Case 2: Don't Buy the House

For a moment, though, let's consider another scenario. Imagine you can only get an 8% APR mortgage from the bank on that $100,000 property, which would put your monthly payment over $750, and you can rent a nice place for much less than that. So, a savvy steward of your finances, rather than putting a down payment of $20k on a house and paying the bank all that "rent," you'd rather invest that money in a broadly diverse index of stocks and rent a home instead over the next 30 years. Maybe you can earn about 8% per year on that $20k investment. And instead of paying your monthly $750+ mortgage payment, you literally pay rent for an apartment or house. How does that compare?

In Fig. 8-4, we can see that our one-time investment of $20k grows to over $200k over the 30 year time period, which is less than the value of the owned home (assumed to appreciate at 3% per year). However, keep in mind that the home value reflects the total payments made every month for 30 years, whereas the stock value has assumed no further investment! On the other hand, the mortgage payment is fixed for 30 years…do you think the rent will go up over that time?

Now, imagine you live in an area where you think property values are in a bubble and are doomed to fall. Or, perhaps you aren't sure you want to live in the same place for 30 years. In the first several years, you'll notice that the Equity and Stocks are not so different (and again, this is assuming you don't continue to invest in the Stocks). In that circumstance, renting for a few years and socking away your money in liquid assets won't be detrimental to your long term net worth.

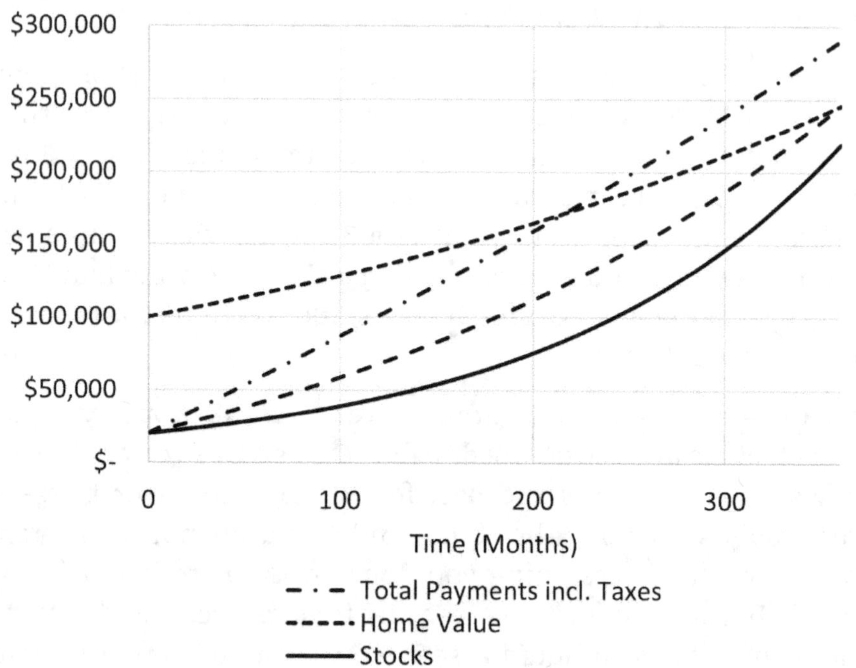

Fig. 8-4 Comparison of Home Purchase and One Time Stock Investment

Case 3: Buy a Smaller House and Invest the Difference

Invariably, when you go to the bank to ask for a mortgage, the price of the house (and the size of the loan) which you are approved for will be large, maybe far larger than makes you comfortable. Good news, right?! We can afford a big house!

Well, let's think about that. In Case 1, we saw that buying the house netted us a stable asset and preserved our net worth over time as the house grew at 3% per year. In Case 2, we saw that investing money with a 30-year horizon and an 8% annual growth rate returned 10x on our initial investment but didn't quite match the home equity in the end.

What if we buy a house, but keep it small and affordable, and invest the rest? Because remember, even when you own a house and it contributes to your net worth, it remains a neutral asset, and you can't really spend it.

So, back to the first example. We bought a $100k house with 20% down, a 6% APR mortgage, 2% local tax rate, and 3% appreciation for the house. We paid $646.31 total every month, and at the end of it all we owned a house worth approximately $250k after paying around $290k total over the 30 years.

In the second example, we invested $20k one time in the beginning and saw 8% growth over the same period. At the end, let's assume we paid $646.31 in rent equivalent to the mortgage payment (fingers crossed they don't raise the rent!), and at the end of it all we owned a stock portfolio with approximately $200k after paying that $290k in an initial $20k investment plus $270k in actual rent over the years.

In this case, let's consider a blended strategy. What if we live a little more within our means? Let's buy an $80k house, with 20% down ($16k), with the same 6% mortgage and 2% tax rate as the first case. But, then let's take the extra money in our budget and regularly invest it in an 8% stock portfolio over the 30 year period. We'll have $4,000 to invest in a stock portfolio on day 1, since our down payment on the house will be $16k rather than $20k. And then every month, we'll take the difference between the amount we would have paid for the $100k house and the amount we're paying for the $80k house and invest it in the stock portfolio.

So the first month, for Case 1, we paid $646.31 in principal, interest, and taxes. For this case, we will pay $517.05, freeing up $95.93 to invest. What happens after that?

You can see in Fig. 8-5 that the house costing 80% to start ends up worth 80% at the end because we've assumed 3% growth for either. So it ends up around $200k instead of $250k. However, that $4k initial investment with continued and disciplined monthly investments over 30 years grows to over $250k. So your net worth is around $450k! You end up with 80% more net wealth by living in a 20% more modest home! And, at the end of the period, those investments will continue to grow exponentially, earning you income in later years.

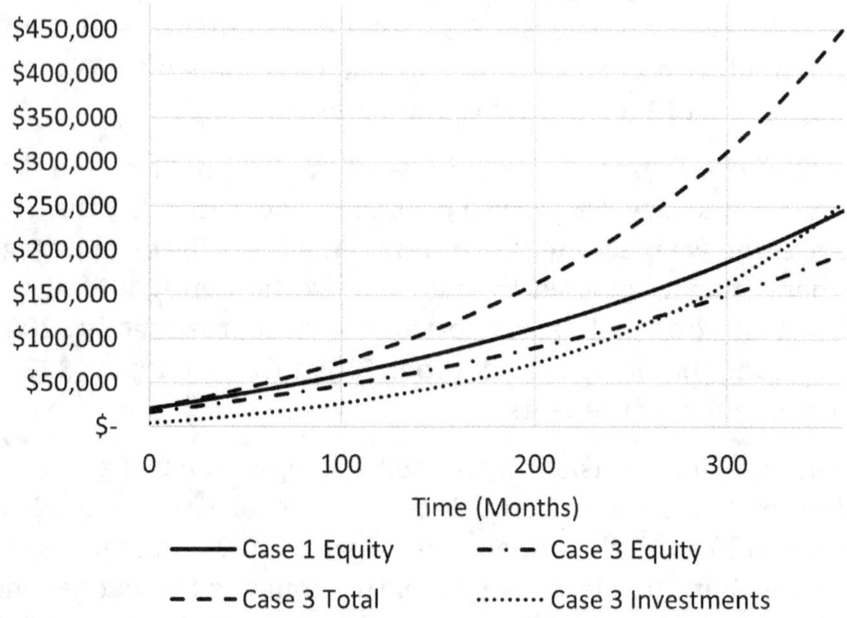

Fig. 8-5 Net Worth from Buying a Home and Investing (Case 3)

This is not magic. Even if your investments only grow at 2% per year, less than the home appreciation of 3% per year, your net worth for this example is $300k. Why? Because the interest and taxes that you pay on the mortgage are gone forever.

Conclusion

So is buying a home a good investment? Is renting better? Well, it depends. In broad strokes, we've found that you should (probably):

- Buy unless renting a comparable space is significantly less expensive or if you expect to move within only a few years

- Buy something well within your budget so you can maximize your investments elsewhere
- Make sure your mortgage interest rate is as low as possible; if you can't get a good rate, consider renting for a few years

Houses, apartments, townhouses, condominiums...there are also intangible benefits of ownership. You might find it appealing to own your home, be able to paint the walls and build a deck. We have found that, in general, smaller and less expensive is better for your net worth (typically). But you literally live your life in this asset, so there is a limit to how far you personally will feel comfortable minimizing the size and cost of your home. In most cases though, if you have a monthly budget available, you will have greater wealth if you spend less than that on your home and invest the difference in a truly appreciating asset portfolio. You will need to find your own balance.

A major note to end this topic: maintenance. In the previous examples we did not include the cost of home repairs and maintenance. Over the 30 year timeline, there will be costs for roof replacements, water heaters, furnaces, air conditioning units, windows, carpets, paint, flooring, landscaping....so buyer beware! A $100k house which is 100 years old and needs everything refurbished might not be as good for your net worth as a brand new $100k house with no big repairs on the horizon This is a wild card, but perhaps another reason to stay on the small and inexpensive end of the market if you are prioritizing your finances.

CHAPTER 9: YOUR BALANCE SHEET

During your early years, your personal balance sheet might be a little messy, and you may have some conflicting decisions to make. You may have some student loan debt. You may have car payments (and of course the corresponding insurance, maintenance, repairs…). You will have rent or perhaps a mortgage loan. How do we reconcile all of that given what we know about investing, tuition costs, mortgage payments, and the overall goal of maximizing assets and minimizing liabilities? Where should our money go?

It can be helpful to use the *rate* of the assets and liabilities as the deciding factor for allocating your resources. The payment (or interest) on a loan with a high rate will be higher, of course. The growth of an asset (investment) will be faster at a higher rate. Since you're on Chapter 9, this is not news to you!

Consider this scenario: You've borrowed $120,000 for tuition and have a government subsidized loan, meaning the interest rate is a low 2%. If you have an extra few hundred dollars every month after paying your bills and making the loan's minimum payment, should you use it to pay off the loan?

Well imagine you can get a guaranteed rate of return on a high yield savings account of 5%. If you instead put that money in the savings account and wait a year, it will have grown more than the 2% you'd owe in interest on the loan. So whatever money you can set aside today in that savings account will be a more effective payment of the loan in a year!

This does not mean that you should spend your money on nonsense other things. This means that you should use the money you have to invest in higher growth assets rather than paying down the very low interest rate loan. Paying off the low interest rate loan is always better than putting it toward a depreciating asset.

Now imagine you have a credit card balance with an interest rate of 25%. Should you pay the minimum payment, or use whatever you can to pay it off as quickly as possible? This is the opposite situation; there is no guaranteed investment that will pay you 25% interest or guarantee 25% growth. So use your money to pay off that debt as fast as you can! And never take on credit card debt again!

When you pay off a loan, it's equivalent to having access to an investment of the exact same rate as the loan.

Back to the mortgage example...if your mortgage rate is 4%, do you want to pay it off as fast as possible, or do you want to use extra available resources for investments? (Remember from Chapter 8 that your mortgage should not consume all of your budget and you should be investing at the same time!) You probably don't want to pay off the loan with extra cash. Over the 30 year horizon, investing extra in your diversified portfolio which can earn maybe 7-8% per year is likely better.

The caveat here is that paying off the loan is equivalent to an investment at that rate, *guaranteed*, whereas investment in something like the stock market is not guaranteed. So the smaller the difference between the loan rate and your expected investment growth rate, and the more uncertain of the investment growth, the more likely it is to be wiser to pay off the loan. And, the shorter the time horizon of the loan, the higher the chances of the investment being a worse decision due to market volatility.

It was previously said in Chapter 2 that all liabilities are bad, but some are less bad, and this is what was meant. On your personal balance sheet, the goal will always be to maximize (appreciating) assets and to minimize liabilities. But it may be advantageous to retain some relatively low interest liabilities so that you can increase the amount of appreciating assets.

Let's look at the example below, expanded from the Chapter 1 example to include a Rate column.

Assets		Rate
Home	$1,000,000	+3%
Stock portfolio	$500,000	+7%
Car	$20,000	-10%
Liabilities		
Mortgage	($500,000)	4%
Student Loan	($120,000)	1%
Car Loan	($10,000)	8%

Assuming you have some spare cash after paying the minimum payments on your student loan, your mortgage payment, and your car loan, the priority would likely be:

1) Car Loan
2) Stock Portfolio
3) Mortgage
4) Student Loan

Notice that the Home and Car assets and their relative appreciation/depreciation rates are irrelevant for your decision-making. They are what they are. Your priority is to maximize your future net worth by reducing your high rate financial liabilities (loans) and increasing your high rate financial assets.

Whether you fully pay off the car loan or simply allocate more to it will depend on the relative rates and the relative certainties... somewhat of a judgment.

What if the car company offered a 0% loan as a sales incentive? Well, that changes everything. In that case, you'd want to pay off that loan as *slowly* as possible, and put any spare cash toward the higher growth investments.

This Chapter is short because the concept is simple. As you regularly invest and allocate funds in the start of your life, just remember to knock out those high interest loans as fast as possible, and try to make yourself comfortable shouldering long term, low interest rate "good debt," like very low rate debt incurred in exchange for education and better earning potential, while you simultaneously build your asset portfolio.

CHAPTER 10: WRAP UP

We've covered the basics of accounting (balance sheets and income statements), different types of assets and liabilities, the differences among assets and how they influence your net worth over time, the basics of stock and bond valuation, the concept of opportunity cost and education investment benefits to your wealth, ways to minimize your risk and costs while benefitting from owning stocks, and strategies for incorporating home ownership into your financial portfolio.

We saw why owning *things* makes you poorer, but owning *investments* makes you richer. Buying those expensive depreciating assets today compounds into missed investment opportunities into the future. Buying investments today compounds into more wealth as your investment keeps working for you.

You learned that the magic of investing comes from starting early and compounding exponential growth for years. You can easily be a corporate tycoon, owning shares of all the huge multinational corporations working on your behalf by owning super low-cost, broadly diversified index funds. Doing so is the easiest way to benefit from the entire US economy while keeping more of your investment earnings to yourself.

We covered how to allocate your investments in tax-advantaged accounts to keep more of your own money. Take full advantage of your employer's 401(k) or 403(b) match, and as you build your investment portfolio, consider IRAs to maximize your long term wealth by minimizing your taxes. If you have access to a pension program, consider yourself lucky and think about participating as a supplement to your own investing.

You learned that minimizing debt and interest payments is always a good thing. And you learned that living modestly when purchasing your home while continuing to regularly invest can have a tremendous impact on your ultimate wealth. At the same time, you learned that relatively low rate mortgage and student loan debt might not be so bad that you need to pay them off ahead of schedule; you can build an investment portfolio while keeping those low rate loans on your personal balance sheet.

That is everything you need to best use your resources and maximize your wealth! Is that everything, though? Well, no. There are a lot of details, and you might want to know more about some things. And you might want to calculate for yourself the consequences of some of your own decisions and strategies. Some things to begin exploring after reading this can be found in the Resources section.

Try not to sweat the details. That trip to the movies won't keep you from being wealthy. But that car and house you stretch your budget for probably will. If you are worried that you can only contribute $3k per year into your IRA, less than the $6500 max, don't be: know you're doing the right thing with that $3k instead of upgrading your collection of gold watches or splurging on the latest diamond-studded iPhone.

Remember that it is easy to have the right financial strategy. Carve out some of your regular income and set up your regular investments. Then forget it, and concentrate on being the best at what you do so that you can maximize your income and your personal career satisfaction.

And if the stock market goes down 15% this year, do not despair, it's an investing opportunity! History shows that the entirety of the US economy is robust and the millions of employees and managers working on your behalf will be successful in the coming years! Remember that you're on the right path and you are setting yourself up for long term success!

RESOURCES

Calculators and Formulae

All of the examples we went over can be replicated with free online tools or by building simple spreadsheets. One easy example is: calculator.net/financial-calculator.html. This website will allow you to calculate loan amounts, project future investment values, see mortgage amortization...

To help with your financial planning and personal budgeting, you might find it helpful to perform calculations to assess your ability to invest, pay a hypothetical mortgage, or even forecast your wealth and retirement situation. The formulas for performing the following may be useful:

Future Value of an Investment:

$$Future\ Value = Principal \times (1 + rate)^{time}$$

Future Value of Regular Investments:

$$Future\ Value = Amount \times \frac{(1 + rate)^{time} - 1}{rate}$$

Monthly Payment on a Loan:

$$Payment = Loan \times \left[\frac{\frac{r}{12} \times \left(1 + \frac{r}{12}\right)^{t}}{\left(1 + \frac{r}{12}\right)^{t} - 1} \right]$$

where r is the % APR and t is the number of months

Financial Data, Stock and Fund Research

Yahoo (finance.yahoo.com) is free and allows you to research stocks, bonds, mutual funds, and major indices. You can look up, for example, the expense ratio of various S&P 500 index funds. You can compare stock and fund performance, explore holdings of mutual funds, find P/E values, almost everything. Google also provides a similar tool (google.com/finance).

Investment Accounts

The major institutions (vanguard.com, fidelity.com) have websites where you can set up your account, research fund options, and more. Once you have an account set up, you can typically add specific types (such as a new Roth IRA account if you already have a personal brokerage account) and link to your bank's checking account. You can set up automatic investments... it's very easy to automatically invest a little bit every paycheck and you'll see your wealth grow!

Gurus and Role Models

Some influential people have dropped nuggets of wisdom over the year, and you can find information from them online or even in books they've written.

Warren Buffet (and Charlie Munger) is famous for being a wise long-term investor and more recently a philanthropist. One of the wealthiest people in the US, Buffett lives frugally and advises on the merits of sustained investment and concepts of fundamental value as we've discussed here. You are unlikely to be led astray financially following Buffett's advice and principles.

John Bogle brought index funds to the masses and founded Vanguard. His book "Common Sense on Mutual Funds" is a must-read if you are not convinced by the examples here about passive index vs. actively managed funds.

There are countless other gurus, some self-proclaimed, who will profess "the way" to become wealthy through cryptocurrencies, stock option trading schemes, junk bonds, or something fast and easy. Be skeptical. Look at their track record. And consider whether there is a long term and fundamental reason to expect returns on your money like you would have when investing in the ownership of profit-earning companies participating in the broader economy.

Account and Tax Information

The IRS website (irs.gov) is relatively easy to navigate to determine the rules for the various types of accounts, including tax rates and contribution limits. As you are investing, it will be important to periodically stay up to date on this information so that you can allocate your investments to suit your needs.

Bubbles and FOMO

We discussed things like cryptocurrency and explained the difference between investments and neutral or depreciating assets. Investments involve contracted or reasonably expected future payment streams.

Cryptocurrencies like Bitcoin, Etherium, Dogecoin…many people have become rich trading them. You may have FOMO (fear of missing out) hearing about that. But they just sit there. They produce nothing, they represent no economic activity. They are not linked to any payment streams. You can only make money if a bigger fool comes along and pays you more for it. For every person making $10 profit on Bitcoin, there is a person who has lost, or will lose, $10.

Do yourself a favor and read about Tulip Mania, during which tulip bulbs became perhaps the first speculative 'bubble' in history. From 1634-1637 tulip bulbs became the subject of wild speculation and became 'worth' typical Dutch salaries. Of course, reality set in eventually and people buying at the height of the bubble lost a LOT. There was no increase in economic output, no productivity gains...just a reshuffling of wealth from some unlucky fools to some other luckier fools.

Sound familiar? Bitcoin at $65,000? Beanie Babies? NFTs? Baseball Cards?

If what you are buying is not related to tangible economic utility, beware!

www.ingramcontent.com/pod-product-compliance
Lightning Source LLC
Chambersburg PA
CBHW070035260726
48658CB00002B/637